NATURE'S FURY

EARTHQUAKE!

Anne Rooney

W
FRANKLIN WATTS
LONDON • SYDNEY

First published in 2006 by
Franklin Watts
338 Euston Road
London NW1 3BH

Franklin Watts Australia
Hachette Children's Books
Level 17/207 Kent St, Sydney, NSW 2000

Produced by Arcturus Publishing Limited,
26/27 Bickels Yard, 151-153 Bermondsey Street, London SE1 3HA

Editor: Alex Woolf
Designer: www.mindseyedesign.co.uk
Consultant: Dr Andrew Coburn

Picture credits:
Corbis: 4 (Bettmann), 15 (Vanni Archive), 17 (Eriko Sugita/Reuters), 18 (Roger Ressmeyer), 19 (Lloyd Cluff), 20 (Patrick Robert/Sygma), 22 (Reuters), 27 (Peter Turnley), 29 (Mimmo Jodice).
Rex Features: cover and 5 (Sipa Press), 9 (Araldo di Crollalanza), 11 (Roy Garner), 13 (Sipa Press), 14 (DigitalGlobe), 21 (Roger-Viollet), 23 (Sipa Press), 24 (Action Press), 26 (Dan Tuffs), 28 (Denis Cameron).
Science Photo Library: 6 (Gary Hincks), 7 (Roger Harris), 8 (Christian Darkin), 10 (Gary Hincks), 12 (Gary Hincks), 16 (Mauro Fermariello), 25 (Peter Menzel).

Anne Rooney asserts her moral right to be recognized as the author of this work.
www.annerooney.co.uk

A CIP catalogue record for this book is available from the British Library

Dewey Decimal Classification Number: 551.22

ISBN-10: 07496 6921 7
ISBN-13: 9780749669218

Printed in China

Contents

What is an Earthquake?

In an earthquake, the ground moves or shakes, sometimes very violently. It can bring buildings crashing to the ground and twist or break up roads, railway lines and bridges. For people who experience an earthquake, it can be a terrifying, dangerous event. A major quake that hits a densely populated area can kill hundreds of thousands of people.

Rippling ground

Shock waves from an earthquake can travel a long way, spreading through the ground just like ripples spread through water. This means that even people living a long way from where the earthquake starts can be affected. Each year the Earth experiences more than 50,000 earthquakes, although most of these are so small they are completely unnoticed by most people and are only detected by scientists using sensitive measuring instruments.

Earthquakes in history

Earthquakes have happened ever since the Earth formed a solid surface 3,800 million years ago. We have historical records of earthquakes throughout human history and geological evidence from earlier times. People long ago did not know what caused earthquakes and often made up legends about them, or believed their gods were responsible for the terrifying events.

▼ *A massive earthquake rocked Tokyo in 1650.*

Danger area

Earthquakes are most dangerous for people when they strike built-up areas. Falling buildings and roads breaking up cause many injuries and deaths. Although there is less danger from an earthquake itself if it happens in open countryside, it can trigger other hazards such as landslides, floods, avalanches and giant waves called tsunamis. These can strike an area already devastated by an earthquake, making rescue operations difficult and killing survivors of the original quake.

THE LEGEND OF NAMAZU

Japan is an area often troubled by earthquakes, and people living there have kept records of them for many centuries. Long ago, Japanese people accounted for earthquakes with the story of Namazu, a giant catfish. According to the legend, Namazu lives in the mud under the islands of Japan. Most of the time the fish is kept still by the god Kashima pressing down on him with the weight of a huge stone. But when Kashima fails to hold him down, Namazu thrashes around and Japan is shaken wildly.

▲ Around 30,000 people may have died when Mexico City was struck by an earthquake in 1985.

Patchwork of Plates

If the surface of the Earth were a single piece, like the skin of an orange, we probably wouldn't have any earthquakes. But it is actually several pieces fitted together like a jigsaw – more like the skin of an orange that has been peeled off and then pieced back together.

Tectonic plates

The hard, rocky surface of the Earth is only the very top layer. It is called the crust. Beneath it is slowly moving, semi-molten hot rock, thousands of kilometres deep. The crust is divided into lots of chunks that fit together to cover the whole surface of the Earth. The chunks are called tectonic plates. There are seven large plates and many smaller ones.

Faults

The lines where tectonic plates meet are called faults. It is along the faults that most earthquakes happen. Most volcanoes are found near faults, too.

▶ *The red dots on this map are often the sites of major earthquakes. Most of these occur at the edges of tectonic plates, shown here in grey.*

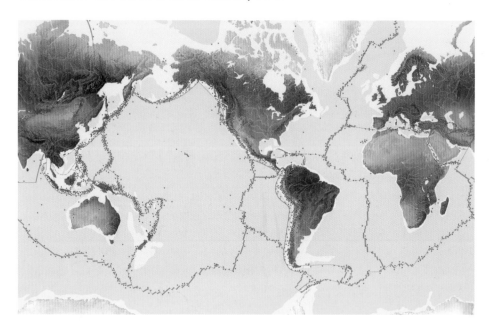

Earth and sea

Six of the large tectonic plates carry land or a mix of land and sea, but much of the Pacific Ocean is on a single, vast plate of its own. The crust that holds land is thicker and older than the crust that carries ocean. Land-bearing crust is also lighter, so it floats higher on the semi-molten rock underneath. The thinner but denser rock of the ocean-bearing crust sinks further into the semi-liquid rock. Because these areas are lower, water runs into them from the higher ground, forming the oceans.

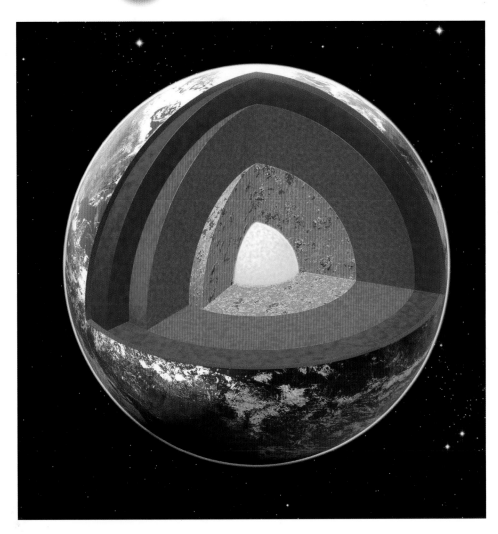

▲ *Beneath the thin surface of the Earth are thousands of kilometres of scalding rock and metal.*

LAYERS OF THE EARTH

The crust makes up less than one per cent of the Earth's thickness. Beneath the crust is a layer of very hot rock called the mantle. The upper mantle, just below the crust, is about 800 degrees Celsius and is almost solid. Below this is the lower mantle, which is hotter – up to 3,000 degrees Celsius – and more fluid. Beneath the lower mantle is the outer core, a thick layer of liquid metal. At the centre of the Earth is the inner core, a ball of metal hotter than the surface of the Sun. Despite its heat, the inner core is kept solid by the immense pressure of the Earth pressing down on it. The very top part of the upper mantle and the crust together are called the lithosphere. This is the part that makes up the tectonic plates.

Moving Lands

The tectonic plates are slowly moving all the time, carried on a layer of thick, gluey, hot rock that gradually creeps around the Earth. They move at around 2.5–15 centimetres per year, some travelling more quickly than others.

▼ *Two hundred million years ago, all the land on Earth was clustered into a single, huge continent.*

Continental drift

The plates carry the land that makes up the continents and the sea floor, so as the plates move, the continents gradually shift around the globe. Over many millions of years, the position of landmasses changes. At the moment, the Atlantic Ocean is growing wider, so North America and Europe are moving away from each other.

Types of fault

Three types of fault are created as plates move in different ways relative to their neighbours. At a convergent (or destructive) fault, tectonic plates push into each other. Over millions of years, land at the edges of one or more of these plates is forced upwards, making vast mountain ranges. The Himalayas, the tallest mountains in the world, began to be formed about 50 million years ago and are still being forced upwards as India moves northwards, pushing into Tibet at a rate of 5 centimetres per year. At a divergent (or constructive) fault, plates move apart and new rock from the mantle comes up to the surface. This is happening in the middle of the Atlantic Ocean and right through Iceland, where hot lava from under the ground forms new land. An area like this is called a rift zone. The new rock forming at ocean rift zones causes the oceans to grow slowly wider. This is called mid-ocean spreading or sea-floor spreading. The Atlantic Ocean is growing by a few centimetres every year.

At a transform (or conservative) fault, plates grind against each other as they move in different directions. There is a transform fault in California, USA, where one plate is moving north and one south. This movement can cause earthquakes. Devastating earthquakes hit California every hundred years or so.

◀ *In Iceland, the mid-Atlantic rift zone is visible on land. Volcanic activity forges new rock and builds new islands.*

NEW CONTINENTS FOR OLD

Around 250 million years ago, all the landmasses on Earth were grouped together in a single vast continent called Pangea (meaning 'all land'). Although the tectonic plates move very slowly – at about the speed your fingernails grow – their movement is relentless. Over millions of years they move enough to reshape the continents completely. Before Pangea, there had been other arrangements of the land. The process has been going on for thousands of millions of years.

Where Earthquakes Happen

Almost all earthquakes happen at faults. Because of this, there are earthquake zones, or places where earthquakes occur repeatedly and where people can expect them to happen.

On the edge

Because the Pacific Ocean is on a large tectonic plate of its own, there are borders with other plates all the way around the ocean. Most of the boundary of the oceanic plate is vulnerable to earthquakes. There are earthquakes on the west coast of the USA, in parts of western South America, and around Japan, eastern China and eastern Russia. Some of these areas – Japan, eastern Russia and parts of Central and South America – also have many volcanoes. The rim of the Pacific is called the Ring of Fire because of these volcanoes.

▼ This diagram shows different types of tectonic fault. The movement of the crust is indicated by the yellow arrows.

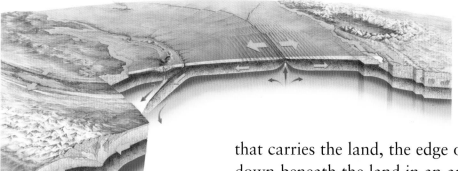

Pushed under

As the sea floor spreads, the plates that carry the ocean are pushed against the plates at their edges. As the oceanic crust is heavier than the crust that carries the land, the edge of the oceanic plate is pushed down beneath the land in an area called the subduction zone. Underground, the old sea floor melts and some of it rises up through the land to burst from volcanoes as lava. Most of the world's land-based volcanoes are in the Ring of Fire.

In the middle

Some earthquakes happen in the middle of landmasses, again where tectonic plates meet. Italy, Turkey, Iran, parts of Russia, northern India and Pakistan are all prone to devastating earthquakes.

Danger zones

Many major cities and communities have been built in areas that are prone to earthquakes. The existence of tectonic plates and fault lines, and their relationship to earthquakes, was not discovered until 1872 when many of the areas had already been settled for hundreds of years.

▲ *A building badly damaged by an earthquake, such as this one in Kobe, must be destroyed before it collapses completely.*

CASE STUDY

Kobe, 1995

Japan is on the junction of three tectonic plates and therefore suffers many earthquakes. On 17 January 1995, an earthquake lasting 20 seconds shook the city of Kobe in southern Japan. The ground moved up to 50 centimetres horizontally and 100 centimetres vertically – enough to topple many older buildings and cause serious damage to new buildings. More than 5,000 people died and 300,000 were left homeless. After the earthquake, fire raged through the city, fuelled by the old wooden buildings.

How Earthquakes Happen

Earthquakes happen because pressure builds up where plates are pushing or grinding against each other. The ground does not move smoothly, but distorts with the tension and finally lurches into a new position, the plates suddenly moving several centimetres or even metres. The tension is released and the ground settles, but over the years tension builds up again, causing another quake.

▼ *Shock waves ripple out from the focus of an earthquake. Above ground, they travel over the surface from the epicentre.*

Before and after

Foreshocks are tremors (small earthquakes) that happen as the ground begins to shift just before a large earthquake begins. Aftershocks happen days or even months later as the plates settle down.

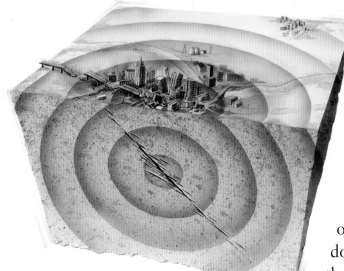

Ripple effect

An earthquake actually happens some way beneath the surface of the Earth, at a point called the focus. The place on the surface of the Earth above the focus is the epicentre. The Kobe earthquake of 1995 was so destructive because the focus was quite close to the surface – only 16 kilometres underground.

Ripples of energy, called seismic waves, spread out from the focus in all directions, including up and down through the Earth. The ground can look as though it has turned to liquid as waves move it up and down like the sea.

An earthquake can have far-reaching effects as seismic waves often spread a long way from the origin of the quake.

Wave after wave

Different types of wave move in different ways and at different speeds. Body waves travel through the Earth, while surface waves spread across the surface. Some types of wave travel up and down; others move from side to side; another type moves like a ripple of energy along a spring. The most damaging, Rayleigh waves, move the ground up and down and sideways at the same time, like waves moving through the ocean.

◀ *The earthquake in Kobe, Japan, in 1995, ripped apart roads and bridges, as well as buildings.*

 CASE STUDY

Antioch, Syria, 526 CE

The earliest earthquake for which written records remain destroyed the city of Antioch in Syria (present-day Antakya, Turkey) on 29 May 526 CE. The quake struck when the city was full of crowds who had come there to celebrate a religious festival. The quake caused oil lamps to fall, sparking a fire that raged through the ruins, killing many people who had survived the quake itself. Records suggest 250,000 people may have died in the city and surrounding area. A large aftershock struck two years later and then another major earthquake in 588.

Sea Quakes

Many earthquakes happen under the sea. Fault lines run all around the Pacific Ocean, along the middle of the Atlantic Ocean and through the Indian Ocean and Mediterranean Sea.

Reaching land

Even if the epicentre of an earthquake is out at sea, the ripples of seismic waves can travel far inland. The shock waves from

► *Aerial photographs show the scene before (top) and after a tsunami hit Banda Aceh in Indonesia in December 2004.*

a very large earthquake can go all around the world, though they get weaker as they get further from the focus of the earthquake. The shock waves may still be strong enough when they reach land to topple buildings. In Europe, a fault runs through the Mediterranean Sea and comes close to southern Italy. Earthquakes near Italy are often felt on the land. In 1908, around 120,000 people were killed by an earthquake in the sea between Italy and Sicily.

Tsunamis

Earthquakes under the sea often cause tsunamis, massive waves that flood huge areas of land. Tsunamis are frequently responsible for more deaths than falling buildings when an earthquake happens beneath or near the sea. A tsunami can even start on a large lake or river.

As the ground beneath the sea moves, a vast body of water drops down or is forced up or sideways, creating gigantic waves which travel in all directions. When the waves approach shallow water, they grow very tall – up to 30 metres – and then they rush inland as a terrible flood, destroying everything. As the wave retreats again, it drags people and wreckage out to sea.

CASE STUDY

Indian Ocean, 2004

On 26 December 2004, a massive earthquake under the Indian Ocean caused a tsunami that flooded lands all around the ocean. Its worst effects were in Indonesia, Thailand, India and Sri Lanka. As part of the seabed near Sumatra was thrust upwards, hundreds of cubic kilometres of water were displaced, rushing outwards in waves that spread over 4,500 kilometres during a period of seven hours, travelling at up to 800 kilometres per hour. At intervals of between 5 and 40 minutes, waves swept up to a kilometre inland, destroying everything in their path. Around 283,000 people were killed.

▲ *The legend of the wooden horse used by the Greeks to capture Troy may refer to an earthquake that destroyed the city – Poseidon, god of earthquakes and the sea, had a horse as his symbol.*

Looking out for Quakes

In the past, foreshocks were the only warning people had that an earthquake might be about to happen. Nowadays, scientists have many ways of watching for possible earthquakes – but we can still be surprised by a quake that gives no warning.

Watching waves

A seismograph is an instrument that picks up movement of the ground, including shifts too slight for us to feel them. In a simple seismograph, a suspended pen draws a line on a piece of paper. As the ground moves, the shaking makes the line wobble – large spikes in the line show significant tremors. Modern seismographs use computers that immediately carry out calculations from the recordings.

A single seismograph can only indicate the distance between the seismograph and the epicentre of a quake – it cannot say exactly where the epicentre is. The epicentre could be anywhere on a circle with a radius of that distance drawn around the seismograph. When information from three seismographs in different places is shared, it is possible to pinpoint the epicentre of a quake. The epicentre is where the three circles drawn around the seismographs cross each other.

Space watch

Seismologists (scientists who study earthquakes) use information from satellites orbiting the Earth to make very accurate measurements of ground movement. Satellites tell them when the ground is shifting or bulging and an earthquake may be on the way. Seismologists can also obtain this information by surveying the land along fault lines. They often use lasers in land surveying to make very accurate measurements.

▲ *Children in Tokyo, Japan, shelter beneath a table during an earthquake drill. The practice will help them to do the right thing if an earthquake strikes.*

ANIMALS AND EARTHQUAKES

There are many tales of animals reacting to an earthquake long before people can feel any tremors. In China and Japan, there are stories of snakes coming out of the ground, of dogs howling, cocks crowing, and even pandas holding their heads in their paws. Before the tsunami that struck Thailand in 2004, elephants headed inland to the forest before the tsunami was visible. Animals appear to be more sensitive to ground movement than people. Sometimes animal behaviour can be used to save human lives. In 1975, the Chinese city of Haicheng was evacuated because of unusual animal behaviour. Several hours later, 90 per cent of the city was destroyed by a massive earthquake.

On the Ground

An earthquake is a terrifying experience for anyone who is caught up in it. The shaking itself lasts only a few seconds, but the damage can be catastrophic.

During an earthquake

The first warning of an earthquake for most people is the foreshocks, which cause windows to rattle and small objects to move around. Sometimes, though, there is no warning and the ground suddenly lurches dramatically. Buildings crack and may fall down, and roads, bridges and railway lines twist and break apart. Damaged structures continue to fall after the shaking stops.

Countryside quakes

Where there are no buildings to fall, the quake is not usually as dangerous for people. The New Madrid earthquake, which struck as a series of shocks in 1811–12, was the largest earthquake recorded on the US mainland. It made huge dips in the ground and formed new lakes, but few people died as it occurred in sparsely populated countryside.

▶ *Houses damaged by the Loma Prieta earthquake in San Francisco, 1989.*

Measuring earthquakes

In order to study and compare earthquakes, seismologists have developed ways of measuring them. There are two methods of measuring the intensity or severity of an earthquake.

The Richter scale applies a number between 1 and 10 to an earthquake depending on the amount of ground movement it causes. Quakes that register below 3 on the Richter scale cannot be felt by people. A severe earthquake measures between 7 and 7.9, and a very severe earthquake measures over 8. Although quakes over 10 could occur, none above 9.5 has ever been recorded.

The Modified Mercalli Intensity scale records levels of damage as a way of comparing earthquakes. The scale goes from I, Instrumental (detected only by scientific instruments) to XII, Catastrophic (with the ground moving in waves, and all structures destroyed).

CASE STUDY

Tangshan, 1976

On 28 July 1976, an earthquake measuring 7.8 on the Richter scale shook the Chinese city of Tangshan. It destroyed 85 per cent of the buildings and probably killed over half a million people in the city and surrounding area, though the Chinese authorities have been reluctant to release accurate figures. It is believed to have been the worst earthquake disaster in recent history in terms of loss of human life. The effects were particularly bad because the city was not built to withstand earthquakes, which are not expected there.

▲ *In 1970, an earthquake in Peru released a massive landslide of debris, which buried the town of Yungay, killing most of the inhabitants.*

Human Catastrophe

The dangers to people of being caught in an earthquake last much longer than the few seconds during which the ground shakes. More tremors and other catastrophes often follow the main earthquake.

Dangerous cities

When an earthquake strikes a built-up area, people may be hit by falling debris, caught in collapsing buildings or trapped under rubble. In a modern city, falling glass and masonry from high-rise buildings pose a threat to people outside, and collapsing ground can crush underground railway networks and bring down road and rail bridges. Flimsy buildings and over-populated cities can lead to a very high death toll. This is a particular danger in South America, the Middle East and the Indian subcontinent.

▼ The tangled wreckage of a railway system, destroyed by the earthquake in Kobe, Japan, in 1995.

Aftershocks

As the ground settles, aftershocks can topple buildings and other structures made unsafe by the main quake. Aftershocks are a serious danger for rescue workers and for people who are trapped or injured and awaiting help. Aftershocks may happen within hours or days, but can occur up to several months after the earthquake.

More disasters

Often, an earthquake triggers further disasters. In towns and cities, damage to gas and electricity supplies can easily lead to fires, which may rage through the wreckage when there are no fire services to fight them and roads are impassable. Landslides, avalanches, mudslides and rock falls are common where there is unstable ground, deep snow or wet land. If sea walls, levees or reservoirs are damaged by the quake, floods can add to the chaos, and areas near the coast may be deluged by a tsunami triggered by the quake.

▲ *San Francisco lies in ruins after the earthquake and fire of 1906.*

CASE STUDY

San Francisco, 1906

The city of San Francisco in California, USA, lies on the San Andreas fault, a boundary between tectonic plates that runs up the western coast of the USA. On 18 April 1906, 430 kilometres of the fault ruptured in a huge earthquake that rocked the city for between 45 and 60 seconds. After the devastation of the quake, the city was engulfed in an unstoppable fire that razed it to the ground. Historians now believe that up to 2,800 people died in the quake and fire.

After the Quake

The after-effects of an earthquake can last for decades, especially for those who lose family members, their home or livelihood.

Immediate aftermath

Straight after a major earthquake, the affected area is in chaos. There are often no communication networks as telephone links and electricity supplies have been lost. There may be no hospitals, no emergency services and no way of getting even basic medical supplies, food and water to survivors.

People who have survived the devastation of the quake may be left without food or shelter, in danger of dying from heat or exposure because they have no protection from the weather and no appropriate clothing.

▼ A boy is helped to safety by a rescue worker after a powerful earthquake in Colombia in 1999.

Public health disaster

Often, the water supply is polluted by debris, spilled chemicals and even the rotting bodies of humans and animals, leaving people without clean water to drink. Disease caused by the lack of clean water and sanitation can spread rapidly through a disaster area and the emergency camps set up to help survivors. It is often impossible for medical supplies to get through if roads and railways have been destroyed, so illness is hard to combat. People with injuries from the quake may not receive treatment, and untreated wounds can quickly become infected.

Wrecked communities

After a major earthquake, many people are bereaved or left homeless, and even more have their way of life destroyed. The local community is robbed of schools, hospitals, workplaces and all the infrastructure of normal life. Individuals may be maimed by injuries sustained in the quake or traumatized by loss, and face a life of struggling to cope with what has happened.

◀ *People pray in the ruins of a mosque in Balakot after the Kashmir-Pakistan earthquake in 2005.*

CASE STUDY

Pakistan, 2005

On 8 October 2005, an earthquake registering 7.6 on the Richter scale hit Pakistan and Kashmir, destroying many towns and villages and causing extensive damage in some cities, including the Pakistani capital, Islamabad. Mudslides and rock falls complicated the situation, blocking roads and leaving many villages and towns cut off from sources of aid. At least 82,000 people died and 3.3 million were left homeless. As winter approached, many survivors were still stranded without shelter or help, cut off by rain and snow, with the dangers of exposure and starvation looming.

Helping Out

The most immediate priority in the wake of an earthquake is to rescue trapped and injured people from the scene. Once rescued, survivors will need food, shelter and medical attention. In major disasters, local, national and international teams work together in the relief effort.

▼ *After an earthquake, survivors may have to live in temporary housing. This city of tents housed people made homeless by the 2005 earthquake in Pakistan.*

First tasks

The danger of aftershocks makes the earthquake zone a dangerous place to stay, so it is important, first of all, to help everyone except rescue workers escape from the area. This can be a difficult task in cases where communication networks and road and rail systems have been damaged, or were poor in the first place, or where roads are blocked by debris or mudslides. In remote areas, helicopters may be the only way to reach people who have been cut off by the disaster. Sometimes supplies must be dropped from planes if it is impossible to get through to people over land.

Emergency relief

People who have been evacuated from the area must be given temporary housing or shelter and provided with food, clean water, clothing and medical treatment. Much effort is put into setting up and running emergency refugee camps. International aid organizations and charities often work together to raise funds and supplies for people who have lost everything.

At the scene

At the site of the earthquake, expert teams and local individuals work side by side to remove rubble and search for survivors. Wounded people must be removed carefully to avoid causing further injury. Rescue workers also face the grim task of removing and identifying bodies. If bodies are not removed and buried rapidly, they can lead to disease.

▲ *The 'blue dragon' robot, used to search for survivors in earthquake rubble.*

TRAPPED IN THE WRECKAGE

After an earthquake hits a city, many people are trapped under the wreckage of buildings. The rubble must be moved carefully, as weakened structures are in danger of falling and killing rescue workers as well as trapped victims. Specially trained search and rescue (SAR) dogs are used to sniff out survivors, and heat-sensitive detectors help to trace people hidden under the rubble. Robotic equipment is used to go into areas too dangerous for rescue workers to enter. Although some people may be pulled alive from the rubble many days after the quake, they have often suffered severe crush injuries and may not always survive.

Rebuilding

▼ *The Transamerica Pyramid building in San Francisco, USA, has been built to withstand powerful earthquakes.*

The impact of an earthquake can last years as a community struggles to return to normal, rebuilding homes, infrastructure and lives.

A new start

Before rebuilding can start, the land must be cleared of all the debris of the earthquake and any unsafe buildings must be pulled down and removed. Not only are new houses needed. Offices, schools, hospitals, shops and other public amenities must all be rebuilt in order for a community to function properly again.

More of the same?

People often want to carry on living in the same place, despite the danger of more earthquakes in the future. A fault can stretch over a long distance, so it may not even be possible to move a community to a safer area.

Where traditional building styles and materials are used, it can be difficult to balance people's desire for traditional homes with measures to make buildings safer in future earthquakes. Safe buildings are also more expensive to build, and some communities are simply unable to afford them.

Building safely

There are several ways of making buildings safer against earthquakes. Most of these methods work by giving buildings a less rigid framework than traditional structures. This allows some movement in the building, so that when an earthquake strikes the building can shake without falling down. In Japan, some structures hang from a central column which is firmly rooted in the ground, but the walls can move when the ground shifts. Other buildings have rockers or shock absorbers built into their foundations. Traditional Japanese houses made of bamboo, wood and thick paper screens fall easily but are less likely to hurt people than brick or stone buildings. They are a fire hazard, though, and many Japanese earthquakes have been followed by disastrous fires.

▲ *A survivor looks at the damage caused by the earthquake in Spitak, Armenia.*

CASE STUDY

Spitak, Armenia, 1988

On 7 December 1988, an earthquake registering 6.8 on the Richter scale destroyed the Armenian city of Spitak and damaged surrounding cities and villages. Because of the building methods used, schools and hospitals were among the worst hit, and many children died. International aid workers and advisors helped in the rescue and rebuilding work, but the Armenians could not afford to make some of the changes recommended. The city has been rebuilt, but could still suffer severe damage in another earthquake.

Where Next?

Although tectonic plates move, faults do not move in relation to the places above them – so the San Andreas fault will always run through San Francisco, and Japan will always be on the junction of three plates. For this reason, the places prone to earthquakes will always be in danger.

▼ *The San Andreas fault in California, USA, is clearly visible from the air.*

Intervals between quakes

Faults do not move, but some are more active than others. In places where the plates move easily, frequent small quakes are felt. Where a lot of stress builds up before the plates finally slip, the earthquake is worse. By studying the intervals between earthquakes in the past and measuring the movement of plates, seismologists are able to say which places may be due for a large earthquake, but they cannot yet predict accurately when an earthquake will happen. San Francisco, for example, can expect a major earthquake in the next 20 years – but that is too vague to help people living in the area.

This table shows the approximate frequency of earthquakes, according to their size:

Richter scale rating	How often?
0.5–2.0	8,000 per day
5	800 per year
7	18 per year
9	1 in 20 years

Evacuation and warning

Some natural disasters are predictable or give some warning, and cities can prepare evacuation plans to help move people out of the area and minimize loss of life. Earthquakes usually strike with no more than a few minutes warning, so evacuation is rarely possible. In places where earthquakes are frequent, people may practise earthquake drills so that they have a well-rehearsed plan of action and can go to a place of relative safety when tremors start. But there will always be surprise earthquakes that seem to come from nowhere, rocking and shattering cities and plunging lives into chaos.

THE POWER OF EARTHQUAKES

Earthquakes can unleash a massive amount of power, which is one reason why we will never be able to control or prevent them. The largest earthquakes – those between 9 and 10 on the Richter scale – unleash the equivalent explosive power of around 1,000 nuclear bombs.

▲ *The bay of Naples, in Italy, is a densely populated area where earthquakes are likely to strike.*

TEN OF THE DEADLIEST EARTHQUAKES

WHEN	WHERE	CASUALTIES
1556	Shansi, China	830,000
1976	Tangshan, China	255,000–655,000
2004	Indian Ocean	283,000
1138	Aleppo, Syria	230,000
1920	Gansu, China	200,000
1927	Qinghai, China	200,000
856	Damghan, Iran	200,000
893	Ardabil, Iran	150,000
1923	Kwanto, Japan	143,000
1948	Asgabat, Turkmenistan	110,000

GLOSSARY

aftershock The shaking of the ground as it settles down after an earthquake.

avalanche A fall or slide of a large body of snow.

convergent fault A boundary between tectonic plates where the plates come together (converge).

core The centre of the Earth, made of molten and solid metal at very high temperatures.

crust The hard, rocky surface of the Earth.

divergent fault A boundary between tectonic plates where the plates separate and new land is formed from lava welling up.

epicentre The place on the surface of the Earth above the point where an earthquake originates.

evacuate Move people out of an area to somewhere safer.

fault A boundary between two or more tectonic plates.

focus The point underground where an earthquake originates.

foreshock The shaking of the ground that comes before the main movement of an earthquake.

infrastructure Large-scale public structures such as power and water supplies, public transport, communications, roads and schools.

lava Molten rock that comes from within the Earth and erupts from a volcano.

levee An embankment alongside a river, built to prevent flooding of the surrounding land.

lithosphere The top part of the Earth's mantle and the crust, which forms the tectonic plates.

mantle The layer of the Earth beneath the crust, made of semi-molten rock.

refugee A person forced to leave his or her home by a natural disaster, war or other event.

reservoir A large area of water collected as a water supply for people.

rift zone An area where tectonic plates are separating.

satellite An object placed in orbit around the Earth in order to provide scientific information.

seismic wave A wave of energy released by earthquake activity.

seismograph An instrument for measuring seismic activity.

subduction zone An area where one tectonic plate is pushed beneath another.

surveying Measuring the lie and position of the land.

tectonic plates Massive chunks of lithosphere (crust and mantle) that make up the Earth's surface.

transform fault A boundary between tectonic plates where the plates slide against each other but ground is neither destroyed nor created.

tsunami A massive wave caused by a disturbance of the sea bed.

volcano A mountain or rift that can emit molten rock (lava) and gases from deep within the Earth.

FURTHER INFORMATION

Books

Explore It: Earthquakes and Volcanoes by Anne Rooney
(Silver Dolphin, 2006)

Eyewitness: Volcanoes and Earthquakes by Susanna Van Rose
(Dorling Kindersley, 2004)

Horrible Geography: Earth-Shattering Earthquakes by Anita Ganeri
(Scholastic, 2000)

Shaky Ground: Earthquakes (Turbulent Planet) by Mary Colson
(Raintree, 2005)

Websites

www.bbc.co.uk/science/hottopics/naturaldisasters/earthquakes.shtm
A quick guide to tectonics and the causes of earthquakes.

http://science.howstuffworks.com/earthquake.htm
A more detailed guide to how earthquakes happen.

www.exploratorium.edu/faultline/activities/index.html
Some activities that help you find out about how earthquakes work.

DVDs

The American Experience: The Great San Francisco Earthquake
(1988; DVD: 2006)

Earthquake directed by Mark Robson (1974; DVD: 2005)

Earthquake: Nature Unleashed directed by Tibor Takacs (2005)

National Geographic: Forces of Nature directed by George Casey
(1999; DVD: 2004)

INDEX

Page numbers in **bold** refer to illustrations.